Dew Drops in Tree Tops

a book of haiku

Gerard Brooker

Illustrated by Tom Phelan

Goose River Press
Waldoboro, ME

Illustrations by Tom Phelan.

Cover photo by Gerard Brooker.

Library of Congress Card Number: 2009934327

ISBN: 978-1-59713-089-9

First Printing, 2009

Published by
Goose River Press
3400 Friendship Road
Waldoboro ME 04572
e-mail: gooseriverpress@roadrunner.com
www.gooseriverpress.com

Dedications

For Dan Sullivan, the best man I have ever known.
And to Sheila, my dear wife,
who is always there for me.
—Gerard Brooker

For my brother William who was lost to us,
but who lives on in my heart.
—Tom Phelan

Dew Drops in Tree Tops

Crickets break the hush
of mid-plains wheat growing.
A small bird warbles.

A star is playing
with limelight and straightrays.
I stand and watch.

Freed from Velcro cling,
hot dried socks flee to daylight.
Running of the bulls.

***

Waiting, waiting now,
oozing, then bursting to life.
Spring is summer sprung.

Picnic in winter,
sun block not necessary.
Stinging bees are gone.

A bluebird never
turns yesterday's tomorrows
into sad todays.

***

Blue paint is always serene.
Purple almost always sad,
coloring the mood.

Dew drops in tree tops.
Far away star winks at me.
So near and so far.

Old squirrel hides nuts
in a safe place on the lawn.
Can't remember where.

It is a cockroach
from the age of dinosaurs.
Basic will to live.

***

They painted it blue,
wanting to compose a mood.
It sticks to my skin.

The tsetse's visit
has gone bad under my lamp.
Time of death: just then.

Her paws are cat knives.
An artist in her own way,
smearing mice on steps.

Dream catcher's snow is
a glimmering shimmering.
We slip on glimmer.

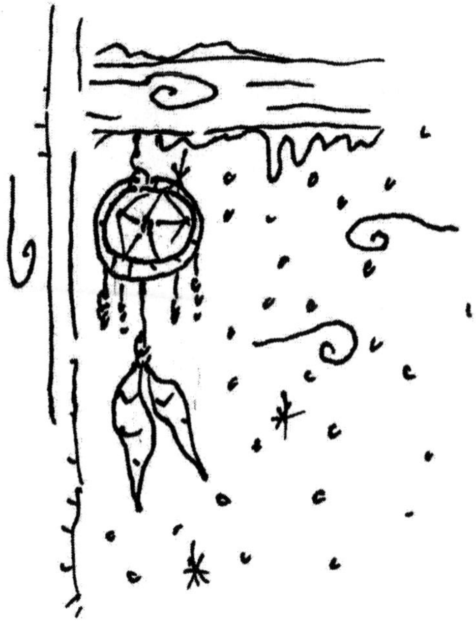

Goo on my left shoe,
two slugs in pachysandra.
Thick gray drool oozing.

This Caribbean.
Cool warm breezes thaw my heart
frozen in winter.

***

It is hard to grasp
the real meaning of this life.
It is what it is.

New spring leaves tingle,
sweet breezes waft by softly.
Buds burst once again.

Hoot-hoot cries the owl
in the starry starry night.
Icon of wisdom.

Bells in the heart,
liberty chimes
pinging, muffled.

I look at the sun
over the Hiroshima bridge.
8:15 a.m.

35

A flashboom changes
into the black rain of night
a bright August day.

Umbra on cement.
Hiroshima Shadow Man
vaporized by heat.

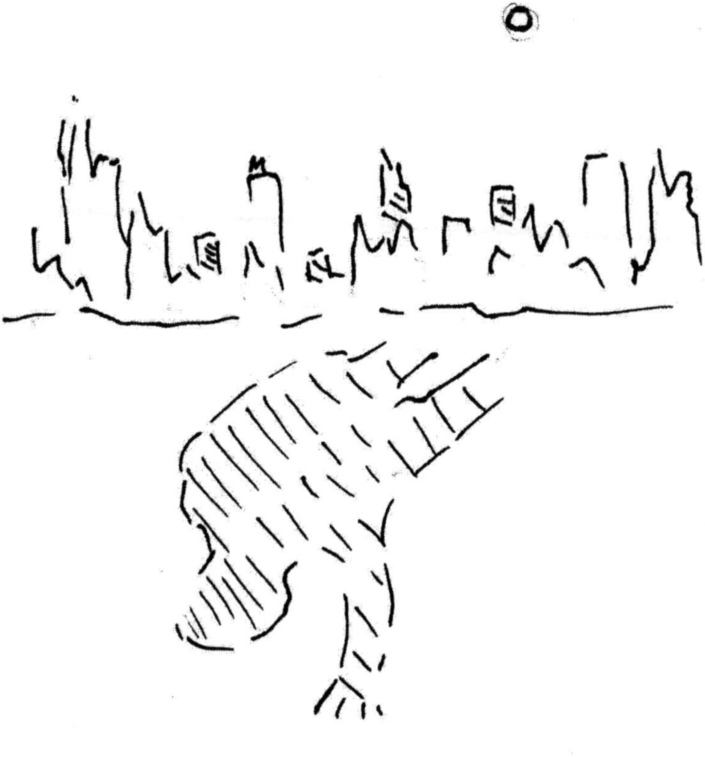

Car wheels over ice,
a knuckle-cracking crunching
neck-role sort of sound.

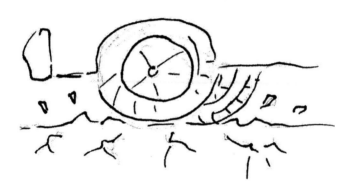

I cannot know you,
mysterious you who are not
always who you are.

***

Four flaps a minute,
hawk time for a thermal.
Ecstasy on wings.

Those who will not play
seed the psychic ulcer with
musketted puffballs.

***

My favorite smells are
like coffee in the morning
forever brewing.

Rain falls hard onto
a dusty city sidewalk.
Smells of the good earth.

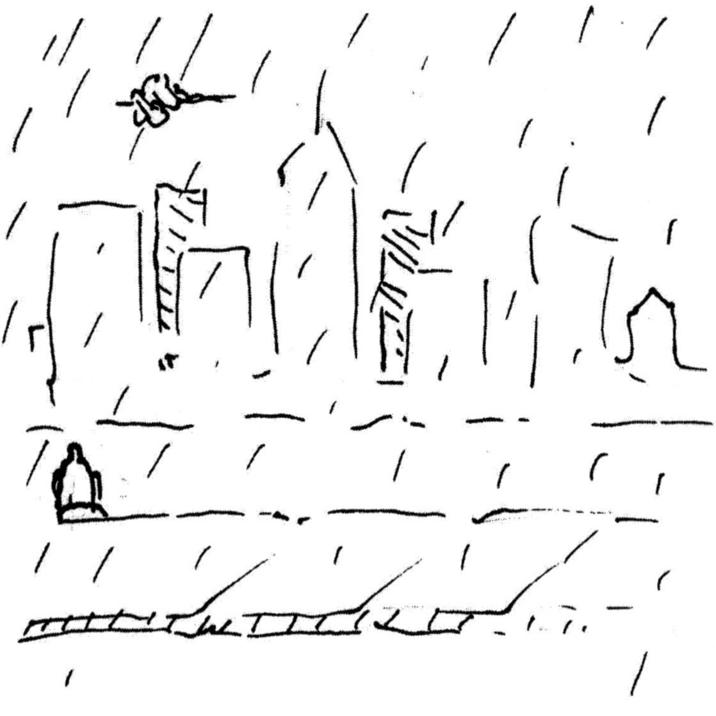

Baked apple pie is
a heavenly scent to me,
adding to its taste.

The chirping of birds
fills air with accord as sweet
as rapping makes noise.

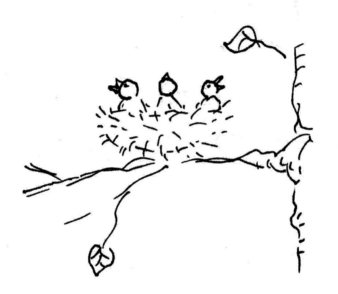

Taste buds salivate.
I yearn for chocolate chunks.
Mouth fills with slobber.

The root of life gives
and then wants to take away.
We try to figure it out.

***

Children are fragile.
Handle them like a Ming vase.
Never press too hard.

A very grave child,
laughter hiding the sadness
no one ever sees.

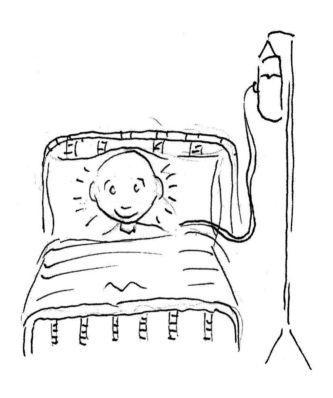

Sometimes, love is
being in the room with her,
breathing in my wife.

You look yummy today.
Sexual harassment?
Not to gummy bears.

Ching clang, chang ching cling.
Clangor of the GNP
ka-chinging along.

***

Soft nips at my hand,
head butts to my overalls.
Tabby clarity.

Today, meaning was
in what was not being said.
Silence had its way.

***

Grains of sand dripping
through slits in hour glasses.
The days of our lives.

I am jittery.
Travel is the opiate
that calms my spirit.

***

Slyly I asked.
No matter, she is the friend
I shall miss this spring.

A clock ticks to end
all living on this planet.
I wait for my tick.

A buddha is born.
Fulcrum event in our time
see-saws back to sin.

Flaking steel rots beams.
Old bridges, spring rains,
falling drops of rust.

All things fall apart.
It is the way of dying
after the hot sun.

I am the good god.
In a winter storm at sea
you will not find me.

The difference between
what is and what ought to be
is often the word.

***

Easy meeting time
quick-slips into heated words.
A wild dog snarling.

Cutting words stick
tension in the room.
My heart is quick-squeezed.

The voice of God speaks
in the green hills of Ireland.
Silk, like smooth sadness.

I am who I am
said the man in the Bible.
Are you who you are?

***

Blunder on blunder
hammerlock words strike on flint.
Mouths that shoot malice.

When you are seven
separation happens fast
as they laugh at you.

***

Expiring plosives.
Spirit flies on heated breath,
killing us bluntly.

Alzheimers is
ants nibbling at the psyche
necessarily.

'Twas the confusion,
the style of obfuscation.
A way to say No.

***

Pathogens amuck
flying through the murky air.
Never touch a muck.

Rock of Sisyphus
falls on innocent children.
Collateral damages.

Some fidget, some stare.
Others read, write or doodle.
The speaker is bad.

Faculty statements
vibrate into thick tables.
Wood cells ooze muddle.

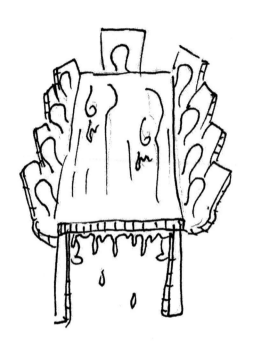

Glitter in the rug.
Precious stone or speck of sand.
I can never tell.

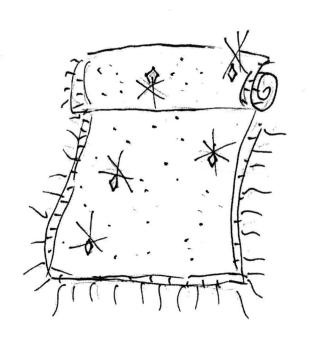

We are what we are.
Could anything be simpler
yet so far removed?